Volcanoes

Sandra Woodcock

Published in association with The Basic Skills Agency

Hodder & Stoughton

A MEMBER OF THE HODDER HEADLINE GROUP

Acknowledgements

Cover: Getty images

Photos: pp iv, 5, 7, 22 Popperfoto/Reuters; pp 8, 17 Mary Evans Picture Library;
p 11 Popperfoto; p 14 Planet Earth

Every effort has been made to trace copyright holders of material reproduced in this book.
Any rights not acknowledged will be acknowledged in subsequent printings if notice is
given to the publisher.

Orders; please contact Bookpoint Ltd, 130 Milton Park, Abingdon, Oxon OX14 4SB.
Telephone: (44) 01235 400414, Fax: (44) 01235 400454. Lines are open from
9.00–6.00, Monday to Saturday, with a 24 hour message answering service. You can
also order through our website: www.hodderheadline.co.uk.

British Library Cataloguing in Publication Data
A catalogue record for this title is available from the British Library

ISBN 0 340 87698 0

First published 2000
This edition published 2002
Impression number   10 9 8 7 6 5 4 3 2 1
Year   2007 2006 2005 2004 2003 2002

Typeset by SX Composing DTP, Rayleigh, Essex.
Printed in Great Britain for Hodder and Stoughton Educational, 338 Euston Road, London
NW1 3BH, by The Bath Press Ltd, Bath.

Contents

		Page
1	The Birth of a Volcano	1
2	What is a Volcano?	3
3	Where are Volcanoes Found?	9
4	The Power of a Volcano	13
5	Living with Volcanoes	19
6	Studying Volcanoes	21
7	The Future	25
8	Some Eruptions	26

This book is about volcanoes. There are many volcanoes all over
the world. This one is called 'The Smoking Mountain'.
It is near Mexico City.

1 The Birth of a Volcano

One day in February 1943
in a small village in Mexico,
a farmer went out into his field.
It was a cold day,
but the soil under his feet felt warm.
He saw a crack in the ground.
It was about 25 metres long.

As he looked at it,
the ground began to rumble.
Smoke and sparks were coming out of the crack.
There was a smell of sulphur.
There was a sound like thunder.
Trees began to shake.

The farmer ran for his life.
As he looked back, he saw red hot rock
coming out of the crack.
He was watching the birth of a volcano.

The next day
there was a cone 10 metres high
where the crack had been.
That day it grew to 45 metres
and red hot melted rock poured from it.
Two villages were wiped out
by the rock and ash that spewed out.
The volcano went on erupting
for nearly 10 years.
By that time it was 410 metres high.
It all began with a crack in a field!

2 What is a Volcano?

Our planet is made up of different layers.
The outside is called the **Earth's crust**.
Men have made tunnels and mines
into the crust of the Earth.

The deepest mines
are the gold mines of South Africa.
It is so hot there,
that the mines have to be made cool
before men can work.
The Earth's crust gets hotter
as you go into it.

Underneath the Earth's crust
it is even hotter.
It is so hot that metals melt – even rock melts.
This melted rock is called **magma**.

Deep in the Earth
very hot gas builds up great pressure.
It can force magma
to the surface of the Earth.

In places where the crust is very thin,
magma can burst through.
When this happens, a volcano is formed.
The hot inside of the Earth is bursting out.
Magma which spills out like this, is called **lava**.

This volcano has steep sides because the lava
cooled quickly.

When a volcano is erupting,
red hot lava, steam, gas and ash pour out.
As the lava cools into hard rock,
it can form a mountain shape.
If the lava cools quickly, the sides are steep.
If the lava cools slowly,
the volcano has gentle slopes.

When the eruption stops
it does not mean that the volcano is safe.
The volcano may be quiet for a time.
It could suddenly erupt again
after a few weeks, months or years.

Just off the coast of Italy,
there is a volcano called Stromboli.
It erupts every 20 minutes.
Some volcanoes are quiet for years and years.
People build houses and farms on the lower slopes.
They live close to the volcano
but the volcano might erupt at any time.

This volcano has gentle slopes because the lava cooled slowly.

Volcanoes like these are live volcanoes.
They are either **active** or **dormant** (sleeping).
If a volcano has not erupted for 10,000 years
it is said to be dead or **extinct**.
In Scotland, Edinburgh Castle is built
on top of an extinct volcano.

Edinburgh Castle (1830).

3 Where are Volcanoes Found?

The Earth's crust feels solid
but it is made up of about 15 huge plates
which fit together like paving stones.
These plates are not fixed.
They are moving.
At points where the plates join,
the Earth's crust is weak.
This is where volcanoes can happen.

Australia is in the middle of a huge plate.
There are no volcanoes in Australia.
However, New Zealand is on the edge of a plate
so volcanoes can be seen there.

The countries most at risk
are around the edge of the Pacific Ocean.
In countries like Mexico, Japan and Hawaii
volcanoes are common.
Sometimes this area around the Pacific Ocean
is called 'The Ring of Fire'.

Many volcanoes are formed in the sea.
Magma forces its way through the Earth's crust
on the floor of the oceans.
These places are called 'hot spots'.

In November 1963,
fishermen near the coast of Iceland
saw smoke and ash rising from the sea.
The water was bubbling, as if the sea was boiling.
Smoke poured thousands of metres into the sky.
The next day there was a new island.

Surtsey is an island which rose out of the sea in 1963.
Fishermen watched the island form from an underwater
volcanic eruption.

The people of Iceland called the island Surtsey,
the name of a god of fire.
At night they watched it glow.
They saw red hot rocks
fly into the black sky.
As the melted rock cooled into hard rock,
the new island grew bigger.

Today Surtsey is 2.6 km square.
Plants, birds and insects live there.
Around the world there are many islands
which were made in this way.
The islands of Hawaii were volcanoes.

4 The Power of a Volcano

Volcanoes have great power.
They can destroy life and change the landscape.
They can kill thousands of people
and destroy whole towns and villages.
Volcanoes have the power
to change the whole planet.
Volcanoes helped to make our planet
long before there was life on Earth.
The power of volcanoes is frightening.

When a volcano erupts,
the lava can do much damage.
Red hot lava flows like a river of fire.
It can destroy farmland and homes.
But lava is not a big killer of people.
It flows slowly,
so people can see it coming.
They have time to get away.

Lava forms a river of fire which can destroy farmland and homes.

If the volcano erupts in a very violent way,
it can throw out big rocks called 'lava bombs'.
Clouds of volcanic ash
can be blown by the wind.
The ash falls many kilometres away.
Most deadly of all
are the fast-moving clouds
of poison gas and red hot ash.
These arc called **pyroclastic flows**.
They can sweep down the sides of the volcano
at 200 km/h (120 mph).
Inside the deadly clouds,
it can be as hot as 800°C.
It is the pyroclastic flows
that kill thousands of people.

In Roman times,
the volcano Vesuvius erupted in this way.
It killed thousands of people
in the town of Pompeii.
Many of them choked to death or were burned.
Ash covered the town.
When the ash cooled and turned into rock,
it set around the bodies of the people.
Their bodies decayed
but the shapes are still there.

Some volcanoes have snow on them.
If they erupt, the hot ash and lava
can mix with the wet snow
to make hot mud flows.
These are like rivers of hot mud.
They flow down the sides of the volcano
and bury everything in their path.

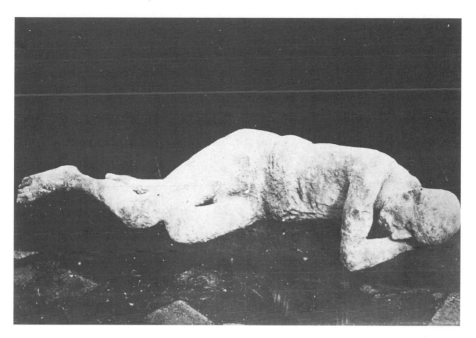

Mount Vesuvius erupted near the Roman town of Pompeii. The shapes of the people who were caught in the volcanic ash can still be seen.

All of these things happened
when Mount Pinatubo in the Philippines
erupted in 1991.
The volcano had been dormant for 600 years.
Ash was thrown 16 km into the air.
400 people were killed.
There were 200,000 refugees.
Rocks as big as tennis balls
hit villages 56 km away.
Day turned into night.
Ash clouds blotted out the sunlight.
The ash settled on villages
in other countries 2000 km away.

5 Living with Volcanoes

Volcanoes are very dangerous
but all over the world
people live very close to them.
Some people live on the slopes of volcanoes.
This is because volcanoes can have
some good effects.

Volcanic soil is very good for farming
because it has lots of minerals in it.
Hot underground magma
can heat water and make hot pools and springs.
In Japan, people like to bathe
in the hot mineral water.
They think it is good for their health.
Some people use small holes full of hot water
as ready-made cooking pots!
In Iceland the heat is used to warm houses.

So in spite of the dangers,
people learn to live with volcanoes.
In Japan, some children go to school
just 5 kilometres from a volcano.
They go to school every day wearing hard hats.
They learn what to do if the volcano erupts.

6 Studying Volcanoes

There are experts who know
a great deal about volcanoes.
They spend their lives studying them.
This is very dangerous work.
They have to go close
to the crater of the volcano.
They collect samples of rock
and measure heat and sounds.
They have to wear special suits
to protect them from the heat.
They use special tools
to take samples from a distance
but they still risk their lives.

Volcano experts checking data on the slopes of Mount Etna.

Studying volcanoes helps them to know more
about the inside of the Earth.
Volcanic rocks tell us about
the history of the planet,
before there was life on Earth.
Experts need to keep watching volcanoes
so they can warn people
if there is going to be an eruption.

Even the experts find it hard
to predict when a volcano will erupt.
The city of Naples in Italy
is very close to Vesuvius.
The volcano last erupted in 1944.
It was a slow eruption with lava flows.
27 people were killed.
Sooner or later it will erupt again.
Next time the eruption
could be a violent one.
There could be pyroclastic flow.
The modern city of Naples
with 400,000 people, could be wiped out.
The experts hope they will get warning signs
in good time, so people can leave the city.

7 The Future

In the past, volcanoes
have made great changes to our planet.
We know that the dust and gases of an eruption
can make changes across the world.

The volcano Tambori erupted in 1815 in Indonesia.
The next year there was so little sunlight in Europe,
that there was no summer.
Really big eruptions could make dust clouds
which block sunlight for many years.
If this happened, all life on the Earth
would be in great danger.
There could be another Ice Age.
The greatest power volcanoes have
is the power to destroy all life on Earth.

8 Some Eruptions

Date	Place	Result
AD 79	Vesuvius, Italy	Two Roman towns destroyed, many people killed.
1669	Mount Etna, Sicily	20,000 people killed
1783	Eruptions in Japan and Iceland	Lower temperatures around the world and a 'Little Ice Age' in Europe.
1815	Tambora, Indonesia	Biggest eruption recorded in history, 90,000 people killed.
1883	Krakatau, Indonesia	Tidal waves caused by the eruption kill 36,000 people.

1902	Mount Pelee in the Caribbean	Pyroclastic flow wiped out the capital city. Only one man survived, 34,000 died.
1980	Mount St Helens, USA	Towns 300 km away had 8 cm of ash, 57 died.
1982	Mount Chichon, Mexico	3,500 people were killed. The sky was dark for 44 hours.
1985	Colombia	34,000 killed
1991	Mount Unzen, Japan	41 killed
1991	Pinatubo, Philippines	400 killed
1997	Montserrat in the Caribbean	Almost destroyed the capital city. The island may be too dangerous to live on.

Glossary of Terms Used

Earth's crust   This is the outer layer of rock which is the surface of the Earth. The part of the earth we stand on.

Magma   Melted rock under the Earth's crust. When great pressure builds up it can be forced out on to the surface. It is then called lava.

Lava   Magma which has come out through the Earth's crust on to the surface of the earth.

Active   A volcano is active it it is erupting or showing signs of erupting.

Dormant   This word means sleeping. A volcano is dormant if it shows no signs of erupting. A volcano may be dormant for a few months or for many years.

Extinct   A volcano which has not erupted for 10,000 years and so is 'dead'.

Pyroclastic flows   These can be seen when a volcano erupts in a violent way. They are clouds of gas and red hot ash which pour out of the volcano. They move very fast (speeds of over 100 mph). Inside a pyroclastic flow it can be as hot as 800°C.